PSALMS

An Invitation to Prayer

A Guided Discovery for Groups and Individuals

Kevin Perrotta

LOYOLAPRESS.

CHICAGO

LOYOLAPRESS.

3441 N. ASHLAND AVENUE
CHICAGO, ILLINOIS 60657
(800) 621-1008
WWW.LOYOLAPRESS.ORG

Nihil Obstat
Reverend John G. Lodge, S.S.L., S.T.D.
Censor Deputatus
October 5, 1999

Imprimatur
Most Reverend Raymond E. Goedert, M.A., S.T.L., J.C.L.
Vicar General
Archdiocese of Chicago
October 7, 1999

The *Nihil Obstat* and *Imprimatur* are official declarations that a book is free of doctrinal and moral error. No implication is contained therein that those who have granted the *Nihil Obstat* and *Imprimatur* agree with the content, opinions, or statements expressed.

The Scripture quotations contained herein are from the New Revised Standard Version Bible: Catholic Edition, copyright © 1993 and 1989 by the Division of Christian Education of the National Council of the Churches of Christ in the U.S.A. Used by permission. All rights reserved. Subheadings in Scripture quotations have been added by Kevin Perrotta.

Joseph Bernardin's reminiscence (p. 21) is from his memoir, *The Gift of Peace* (Chicago: Loyola Press, 1997).

Dorothy Day's reminiscence (p. 31) is from her memoir, *From Union Square to Rome* (Silver Spring, Md.: Preservation of the Faith Press, 1939), available at the Dorothy Day Library on the Web at www.catholicworker.org/dorothyday.

Margaret Kennedy's story (p. 51) originally appeared in *God's Word Today* magazine.

The Latin text of the excerpt from a sermon by Bernard of Clairvaux (p. 61) can be found in *Sermones super Cantica Canticorum*, edited by Jean Leclerq et al. (Rome: Editiones Cistercienses). Translation by Kevin Perrotta.

The Latin text of the excerpt from a sermon by Augustine (p. 71) can be found in *Patrologia Latina*, edited by J. Migne. Translation by Kevin Perrotta.

Interior design by Kay Hartmann/Communique Design
Illustration by Charise Mericle Harper

ISBN 0-8294-1434-7

Printed in the United States of America
05 06 07 08 09 10 Bang 10 9 8 7 6

Contents

How to Use This Guide

You might compare this booklet to a short visit to a national park. The park is so large that you could spend months, even years, getting to know it. But a brief visit, if carefully planned, can be enjoyable and worthwhile. In a few hours you can drive through the park and pull over at a handful of sites. At each stop you can get out of the car, take a short trail through the woods, listen to the wind blowing in the trees, get a feel for the place.

In this booklet we'll drive through the book of Psalms, making half a dozen stops along the way. At those points we'll proceed on foot, taking a leisurely walk through the selected passages. The readings have been chosen to give a representative sample of the various kinds of prayers contained in the book of Psalms. These passages will bring us to the heart of the psalmists' relationship with God. After each discussion we'll get back in the car and take the highway to the next stop.

This guide provides everything you need to explore the book of Psalms in six discussions — or to do a six-part exploration on your own. The introduction on page 6 will prepare you to get the most out of your investigation of the psalms. The weekly sections feature two psalms, with explanations that highlight what these prayers mean for us today. Equally important, each section supplies questions that will launch you into fruitful discussion, helping you both to explore the psalms for yourself and to learn from one another. If you're using the booklet by yourself, the questions will spur your personal reflection.

Each discussion is meant to be a *guided discovery*.

Guided. None of us is equipped to read the Bible without help. We read the Bible *for* ourselves but not *by* ourselves. Scripture was written to be understood and applied in and with the church. So each week "A Guide to the Reading," drawing on the work of both modern biblical scholars and Christian writers of the past, supplies background and explanations. The guide will help you grasp the meaning of the psalms. Think of it as a friendly park ranger who points out noteworthy details and explains what you're looking at so you can appreciate things for yourself.

Discovery. The purpose is for *you* to interact with the psalms and make them part of your own prayer life. "Questions for Careful Reading" is a tool to help you dig into these ancient prayers and examine them carefully. "Questions for Application" will help you consider what the psalms mean for your relationship with God here and now. Each week concludes with an "Approach to Prayer" section that launches you into praying the psalms with deeper meaning. Supplementary "Living Tradition" and "Saints in the Making" sections offer the thoughts and experiences of Christians past and present in order to show you the impact the book of Psalms has had and is having on other people—so that you can consider what it might mean for you.

How long are the discussion sessions? We've assumed you will have about an hour and a half when you get together. If you have less time, you'll find that most of the elements can be shortened somewhat.

Is homework necessary? You will get the most out of the discussions if you read the weekly material in advance of each meeting. But if participants are not able to prepare, have someone read the "Guide to the Reading" section aloud to the group at the points where it occurs in the weekly material.

What about leadership? If you happen to have a world-class biblical scholar in your group, by all means ask him or her to lead the discussions. But in the absence of any professional Scripture scholars, or even accomplished biblical amateurs, you can still have a first-class Bible discussion. Choose two or three people to be facilitators, and have everyone read "Suggestions for Bible Discussion Groups" before beginning (page 76).

Does everyone need a guide? a Bible? Everyone in the group will need their own copy of this booklet. It contains the psalms that are discussed, so a Bible is not absolutely necessary—but each participant will find it useful to have one. You should have at least one Bible on hand for your discussion. (See page 80.)

How do we get started? Before you begin, take a look at the suggestions for Bible discussion groups (page 76) and individuals (page 79).

Psalms: An Invitation to Prayer

From the moment of our conception, an unseen Person has accompanied us through our life. He was at the bedside when we were first placed in our mother's arms.* On every playground where we played, by every classroom desk we sat in, at every table where we ate, he has been with us. He has been there as we worked, as we loved, as we shopped. He has been with us in the moments when we were kind and caring to others — and no less present when we treated others shabbily and unfairly. At all times he has gazed into the murky depths of our heart and has seen our intentions as clearly as brightly colored fish darting before the eyes of a snorkeler in transparent Caribbean waters.

Our divine Companion wants us to know him as intimately as he knows us. God's hope is that, when we reach the end of our earthly life and are thrust by death into eternity, we will see him gazing at us with tender love, as we saw our mother gazing down at us in the hour we were born. The hours of our life — varied jewels strung on a thread stretching between birth and death — are a series of opportunities to become aware of him. Whether we feel him to be near or far, whether his voice resounds or seems to have fallen silent, each hour is a chance to turn our attention to him, to grip his unseen hand and step forward on the path that will bring us to his face.

The Companion of our life is always listening. Depending on the phase of our life's journey, God invites us to celebrate his love, ask his help, seek his forgiveness, or declare our trust in him. God waits to hear the expression of our heart.

But, speaking for myself, there is a problem here. My life is a jumble. I do not always know my own heart. Often I do not notice my blessings or recognize my deepest needs. Even when I do, I fumble for words. Most days I am too distracted to say much

* God, of course, is neither male nor female. I am using the traditional masculine personal pronouns for God to avoid the impersonal tone produced by rigorously avoiding the use of personal pronouns in reference to God. While the Bible often uses masculine metaphors for God, it also uses feminine ones — as in this image from Psalm 131 that compares God to a mother gazing down at her baby.

to my Companion. Besides, my mental picture of him is, I constantly discover, woefully inadequate. For many reasons, I need help to pray.

People have long felt this need. The oldest writings in the world — those of the ancient Near East — contain many prayers. These prayers were written down to show people how to pray. But not all help is helpful. Inscriptions addressed to the ancient gods Marduk, Ishtar, and Enlil are interesting but not usable. We need prayers that help us speak to our life Companion as he really is.

We would be most helped if our Companion offered suggestions for our prayers on the basis of his unimpaired knowledge of himself and us. Happily, this is just what he has done. More than three thousand years ago God brought a Near Eastern people called Israel into a special relationship with him. Over time, he rescued them from many evils and instructed them in how to live well. Guided by God to hear his voice and discern his hand in their lives, the people of Israel discovered him to be merciful, faithful, and just. In response, they learned to talk with their Lord trustingly about the whole range of their experience. As they passed through the lights and shadows of life, they praised their mysterious Companion and appealed to him. They spoke to him heart to heart.

At temple festivals, in smaller groups, and in solitude, the Israelites sang their prayers to God. The song-prayers were written, rewritten, sifted, collected. At the conclusion of the process, 150 prayers of the people of Israel filled a book, which was then shelved in the library Christians call the Old Testament. That book of prayers is the book of Psalms — Israel's collection of prayers for singing to God.

Shaped in the dialogue between the people of Israel and their divine Companion, the psalms communicate a vision of God as the Companion of our life. Indeed, the opening paragraphs of this introduction basically restate the outlook of the book of Psalms (compare Psalms 17:15; 63:5 – 8; 121; 131; 139). The psalms are a God-given resource for prayer — God's invitation to us to speak with him. They express the whole span of human experience in the presence of God: joy and pain, love and hate, peace and dread, exultation and desperation. It has even been said that there is a psalm for every situation. In a general way that is true, although there is no specific psalm to pray while driving to your wedding or after completing the deck on your house.

But a question arises. Are Old Testament prayers still usable, now that God has shown himself in his Son? We want to pray to God as he has fully revealed himself. The Old Testament bears witness to God's dealings with his chosen people before Jesus of Nazareth. Once we have recognized that our life's Companion has most fully revealed himself in Jesus, can we still pray the psalms?

Jesus, of course, is the best person to deal with this question. And while the Gospels do not quote him on this precise question, they show us the answer. On one occasion Jesus' disciples asked him to teach them to pray. He obliged them by giving them the Our Father, or Lord's Prayer (Matthew 6:9–13; Luke 11:2–4). But the Our Father is a single prayer, not an entire prayer book; it is a model for prayer, not a replacement of all other prayers. Significantly, Jesus continued to pray the psalms. At the end of the Last Supper he sang the traditional psalms for the Passover meal with his disciples (Mark 14:26). On the cross he cried out to his Father in the words of Psalm 22: "My God, my God, why have you forsaken me?" (Mark 15:34). Apparently Jesus intended his followers to go on using the psalms. Judging from references in the New Testament, that is what the early Christians did (Ephesians 5:19; Colossians 3:16).

Thus Jesus pointed us toward both the book of Psalms and the Our Father. We may use the Our Father as Jesus' way of showing us where to put the emphasis when we pray the psalms. To put it another way, the Our Father gives us Jesus' agenda for prayer, while the psalms provide us with material for carrying it out.

In this booklet, then, the prayer that Jesus taught us will provide the plan for our exploration of the book of Psalms. Our discussions will follow this sequence:

✦ "Our Father, who art in heaven, hallowed be thy name." We will begin with psalms that acclaim God's reign (Week 1).

✦ "Thy kingdom come, thy will be done, on earth as it is in heaven." We will move on to psalms that call on God to restore his people and bring justice to the world (Week 2).

✦ "Give us this day our daily bread." We will turn to psalms that present our individual needs to God (Week 3).

✦ "Forgive us our trespasses, as we forgive those who trespass against us. And lead us not into temptation, but deliver us from evil." Next come psalms asking God to forgive us and enable us to be faithful to him (Week 4).

✦ The Lord's Prayer does not explicitly give thanks. But when God shows us his mercy and kindness, it is natural to thank him. So we will read psalms of thanksgiving (Week 5).

✦ We will conclude by returning to the beginning of the Lord's Prayer: "Our Father." These words of deepest trust point us to psalms that express confidence and hope in our Companion (Week 6).

The psalms can sustain and deepen our relationship with our Companion—just as they sustained Jesus' relationship with God from his boyhood in Nazareth to his final moments on Golgotha.

The psalms are a kind of quarry from which we can extract prayers that put into words what we wish to say to God. But there is another side to the psalms. Some of the material in the psalms is different from what we might wish to say to God. Parts of the psalms are difficult to understand; parts are even disturbing.

This should not be surprising. The men and women who first prayed the psalms lived long ago in a world quite different from ours. They never turned a key in the ignition of a car or clicked the mouse of a computer. They lived in small stone houses, tended sheep and goats, and raised barley and olives. When the sun went down, they stopped working and slept under a majestic night sky unobscured by electric lights. Of course, in their basic humanity they were just like us. They related to the same divine Companion we do. But culturally they were a million miles from us. We can't expect their prayers to be exactly like ours.

Moreover, the composers of the psalms lived in an earlier phase of God's revelation than we do. There were many things they did not have the advantage of knowing. That sickness is not usually a symptom of sin, that there will be a resurrection of the dead and reward and punishment in a life to come, that God wishes to save not only Israel but also the whole human race — these realities had hardly begun to dawn on the psalm writers.

Thus while many lines in the psalms are easily accessible to us, others strike us as foreign. Consequently, effort is required to read the psalms with understanding. Not everything is clear at first. Not everything is clear even after much study.

So how should we proceed? Here are two suggestions: First, begin to pray the parts of the psalms that are easy to understand and that fit your needs. Second, be open to learning from what is unfamiliar.

Beginning with the familiar means locating the parts of the psalms that, without further study, make it easier for us to express ourselves to God. For example, when we are inclined to praise God, the exuberance of Psalm 96, which imagines forests of trees singing to God, might help put our mood into words (96:12 – 13). The psalmist's description of grief in Psalm 6 leaps the centuries to describe our own experience: "I am weary with my moaning; every night I flood my bed with tears" (6:6). Without further ado Psalm 51:9 expresses our plea that God would forgive and forget the times we have turned from him: "Hide your face from my sins, and blot out all my iniquities." We may easily resonate to lines like these. Let us weave them into our conversation with God.

Being open to learning means expecting that what is strange may convey wisdom. The psalmists, for example, try to persuade God to act — an approach that may seem odd to us. But if we probe their arguments, we will discover that the psalmists model a deep trust in God. If we explore the parts of the psalms that are uncomfortable to us, we will find elements of prayer and faith that may enlarge and reshape our own relationship with God. In a sense, the psalms are a workshop that trains us in prayer, and often the aspects of the psalms that strike us as different contain the training.

The more we explore and ponder the psalms, the more they will deepen our relationship with God. The psalms were the prayers of Israel in dialogue with God in the centuries before Jesus. They were the prayers of Jesus. They have always been the chief prayers of the Church. In the view of the early teachers of the Church, such as St. Augustine, the psalms remain the prayers of the glorified Jesus because he continues to pray them through us, the human members of his body. Indeed, with mysterious, multilayered meanings, the psalms speak prophetically of Jesus (Luke 24:44).

Let us, then, explore the book of Psalms, so that we may speak more intimately with our Companion.

HALLOWED BE THY NAME

Questions to Begin

15 minutes
Use a question or two to get warmed up for the reading.

1 What is your favorite prayer? Why?

2 What is your favorite style of prayer?
- ❑ Being silent in God's presence
- ❑ Having a private conversation with God
- ❑ Praying informally with friends
- ❑ Celebrating the liturgy with contemporary songs
- ❑ Celebrating the liturgy with some Latin and traditional hymns
- ❑ Keeping a journal
- ❑ Praying with Scripture

5 minutes
Read the psalms aloud. Let individuals pray successive verses,
or divide into two groups and pray the verses alternately.

The First Priority

"Hallowed be thy name." Behind these obsolete English words lies
an up-to-date meaning: "May you, God, act so that people will
acknowledge you as the great, merciful, wise, trustworthy God
that you are!" Jesus summons us to begin our prayer by focusing
on God rather than on ourselves, to recognize God's agenda before
presenting our own. So we begin with two psalms of praise.

The Reading

Psalm 96: Hey, Everybody, Acknowledge God!

1 O sing to the LORD* a new song;
  sing to the LORD, all the earth.
2 Sing to the LORD, bless his name;
  tell of his salvation from day to day.
3 Declare his glory among the nations,
  his marvelous works among all the peoples.
4 For great is the LORD, and greatly to be praised;
  he is to be revered above all gods.
5 For all the gods of the peoples are idols,
  but the LORD made the heavens.
6 Honor and majesty are before him;
  strength and beauty are in his sanctuary.
7 Ascribe to the LORD, O families of the peoples,
  ascribe to the LORD glory and strength.
8 Ascribe to the LORD the glory due his name;
  bring an offering, and come into his courts.
9 Worship the LORD in holy splendor;
  tremble before him, all the earth.
10 Say among the nations, "The LORD is king!

* The translators use an uppercase L and small capital letters for the rest of
the word to indicate that the Hebrew text uses not the Hebrew word for lord
but the proper name of God ("Yahweh").

The world is firmly established; it shall never be moved.
He will judge the peoples with equity."
11 Let the heavens be glad, and let the earth rejoice;
let the sea roar, and all that fills it;
12 let the field exult, and everything in it.
Then shall all the trees of the forest sing for joy
13 before the Lord; for he is coming,
for he is coming to judge the earth.
He will judge the world with righteousness,
and the peoples with his truth.

Psalm 111: Remember What God Has Done

1 Praise the LORD!
I will give thanks to the LORD with my whole heart,
in the company of the upright, in the congregation.
2 Great are the works of the LORD,
studied by all who delight in them.
3 Full of honor and majesty is his work,
and his righteousness endures forever.
4 He has gained renown by his wonderful deeds;
the LORD is gracious and merciful.
5 He provides food for those who fear him;
he is ever mindful of his covenant.
6 He has shown his people the power of his works,
in giving them the heritage of the nations.
7 The works of his hands are faithful and just;
all his precepts are trustworthy.
8 They are established forever and ever,
to be performed with faithfulness and uprightness.
9 He sent redemption to his people;
he has commanded his covenant forever.
Holy and awesome is his name.
10 The fear of the LORD is the beginning of wisdom;
all those who practice it have a good understanding.
His praise endures forever.

10 minutes
Choose questions according to your interest and time.

---

1   What clues can you find to indicate who is praying in these psalms and where they might be praying?

---

2   In each psalm, who is being spoken to?

---

3   What is the main point the psalmist is trying to express in each of these psalms?

---

4   How would you describe the psalmist's mood, his attitude toward his situation?

---

5   What reasons does the psalmist give for praising God? (Look for statements that begin with words such as *because, for, since, so that,* or *therefore.*)

A Guide to the Reading

If participants have not read this section already, read it aloud. Otherwise go on to "Questions for Application."

The Israelites sang Psalm 96 in the liturgy of the Jerusalem temple (notice 96:8). This psalm resounds with the people's amazement at God's grandeur and their awe at his presence with them (96:8–9). Sure, other nations have their gods (96:4), but those gods are nothings, nobodies (96:5). Israel's God is the real God, for he made the earth (96:10) and the rest of the universe too (96:5). His people in the temple courtyard, the rest of the human race, and even hills and forests should sing his praises. And let the seas accompany the chorus with thundering surf (96:11). Hallowed, hallowed be his name!

Psalm 111 suggests the more subdued atmosphere of an author's study or a teacher's classroom. The lines begin with successive letters of the Hebrew alphabet — a project that must have kept the author working quietly at his desk for quite some time. Ronald Knox's translation conveys the effect:

> **A** ll my heart goes out to the Lord in praise,
> **b** efore the assembly where the just are gathered.
> **C** hant we the Lord's wondrous doings. . . .

Verse 10 sounds like a teacher's instruction, which is a reason for thinking that this psalm was designed for a school of some sort. Of course, depending on the mix of personalities, classrooms can be pretty noisy too!

Loudly or softly, both psalms praise God — and lead us to reflect on what praising God means.

Praise itself is no mystery. It is our natural response to excellence. What football crowd sits in silence when a quarterback throws a touchdown pass? To praise God is ultimately to become lost in wonder at God's excellence. The *Catechism of the Catholic Church* tells us that praise of God honors God not just for what he does for us but also "for his own sake . . . simply because he is" (section 2639). Obviously, though, we reach this exalted amazement at who God is through the good things God does for us. It is when we experience God helping us, guiding us, rescuing us, forgiving us, healing us, and giving us peace that we discover how wise, powerful, and kind he is. We climb up to a state of wonder-filled praise of God on the rungs of a ladder that consists of his acts of kindness and mercy toward us.

But if we are to mount up to perfect praise of God, it is crucial for us to recognize and remember the ways that God helps us, guides us, and so on. If we do not notice what God does, or if we forget, then our inclination to praise him withers.

On this point, the psalms set a tremendous example, for the psalmists are constantly remembering the good things God has done. Psalm 96 speaks of God's "marvelous works" (96:3), that is, his creation of the earth and the heavens (96:5, 10). Psalm 111 reminds us of the miracles by which God freed the Israelites from slavery in Egypt ("his wonderful deeds" — 111:4), his supplying their needs during their desert journey (111:5), his settling them in Canaan (111:6). (God's great works in 111:2 made St. Jerome, the fourth-century biblical scholar, think of the creation of elephants and camels!) The psalmists are like sports announcers who impress us with the quarterback's record-breaking statistics as we watch the team lining up for a play. Because the psalmists are constantly remembering God's deeds, they are constantly praising him.

In fact, for the psalmists, God's actions are both the reason for praising him and the content of the praise. Psalm 96 gives God's mighty actions as the motivation for praise: "Sing to the LORD . . . *for* . . . the LORD made the heavens" (96:2–5, italics mine). But both Psalms 96 and 111 praise God simply by reciting what God has done for his people. God's deeds provide both the motive for singing to him and the lyrics of the song.

The early Christians continued to praise God by recalling what he has done. They "composed hymns and canticles in light of the unheard-of event that God accomplished in his Son: his incarnation, his death which conquered death, his resurrection, and ascension to the right hand of the Father" (*Catechism,* section 2641). So we pray Psalm 96 to celebrate God's reign through Jesus, rejoicing in the coming of the Lord who reigns already and looking forward to his final coming, when he will bring God's kingdom to completion (96:10–13).

Questions for Application

40 minutes
Choose questions according to your interest and time.

---

1 Where is the balance between praising God and asking God for what we need?

---

2 What part does praising God have in your prayer? How could you make praising God a higher priority?

---

3 What one or two events in your life have most clearly shown you God's mercy and love? How often do you remember these actions of God when you pray? What could you do to recall these moments of particular grace and to praise God for them?

---

4 Psalm 96 suggests that we praise God not only by recalling his actions when we are gathered in the liturgy but also by telling other people about him. In what ways do you let the people you live with and work with know about what God has done for you? about what he has done for everyone in the coming of his Son? How could you praise God more in this way?

5 Does God gain anything from our praise? Do we?

6 What line from either of these psalms would you like to make a part of your own prayer? Why?

"During the meeting a candle could be lighted to remind us that when we are reading the Bible, Christ is present in our midst and God our Father is speaking to us."

James Rauner, *The Young Church in Action*

Approach to Prayer

15 minutes
Use this approach — or create your own!

✦   Read aloud Philippians 2:5 – 11;
Colossians 1:15 – 20; and Titus
3:4 – 7, pausing for a minute of
silent reflection after each reading. Then pray together Psalm
96 in praise of God for the
coming of his kingdom.

End with the Our Father.

Saints in the Making

Giving God Quality Time

This section is a supplement for individual reading.

I discovered that I was giving a higher priority to good works than to prayer." That statement could be made by many Christians. In this case it was made by Joseph Bernardin, who at the time was the Catholic archbishop of Cincinnati. "It was not that I lacked the desire to pray or that I had suddenly decided prayer was not important. Rather, I was very busy, and I fell into the trap of thinking that my good works were more important than prayer."

One evening at dinner Cardinal Bernardin spoke with some younger priests about his lack of prayer. "In very direct — even blunt terms — they helped me realize that I was urging a spirituality on others that I was not fully practicing myself. These priests helped me understand that you have to give what they called 'quality time' to prayer. It can't be done 'on the run.' You have to put aside good, quality time. After all, if we believe that the Lord Jesus is the Son of God, then of all persons to whom we give ourselves, we should give him the best we have."

Bernardin resolved to spend the first hour of each day in prayer. "I said, 'Lord, I know that I spend a certain amount of that morning hour of prayer daydreaming, problem-solving, and I'm not sure that I can cut that out. I'll try, but the important thing is, I'm not going to give that time to anybody else. So even though it may not unite me as much with you as it should, nobody else is going to get that time.'"

As part of his prayer, Bernardin would pray the Liturgy of the Hours, a traditional Catholic format for daily prayer. "A major portion of the prayers are from the Psalms. I have found the Psalms to be very special because they relate in a very direct, human way the joys and sorrows of life, the virtues, the sins. They convey the message that good ultimately wins out. And as you see the people who are mentioned in the Psalms struggling to be united with the Lord, it gives you encouragement."

Cardinal Bernardin, who served as archbishop of Chicago, died in 1996.

THY KINGDOM COME

Questions to Begin

15 minutes
Use these questions to prepare for the reading and discussion.

1 What are the chief problems facing your parish community as you attempt to follow the Lord? For example, problems such as these may come to mind:

+ The demands of earning a living make people so busy it is difficult to find time to pray or take part in parish activities.

+ Non-Christian influences in the media and elsewhere compete with parents' influence over children.

2 In your opinion, what areas are most in need of strengthening? What makes these areas especially important? What are the obstacles to renewal? Make a short list, and hold on to it for later in the discussion.

5 minutes
Read the psalms aloud. Let individuals pray successive verses,
or divide into two groups and pray the verses alternately.

God, Set Things Right!

"Thy kingdom come, thy will be done, on earth as it is in heaven."
With these words, Jesus urges us to call on God to bring justice,
healing, and reconciliation into our world. The psalms provide
us with plenty of material for appealing to God to set things right
in the world and to care for his people. This week we look at two
of these psalms.

The Reading

Psalm 10: The Powerful Prey on the Weak

1 Why, O LORD, do you stand far off?
  Why do you hide yourself in times of trouble?
2 In arrogance the wicked persecute the poor —
  let them be caught in the schemes they have devised.
3 For the wicked boast of the desires of their heart,
  those greedy for gain curse and renounce the LORD.
4 . . . the wicked say, "God will not seek it out";
  all their thoughts are, "There is no God." . . .
8 They sit in ambush in the villages;
  in hiding places they murder the innocent.
  Their eyes stealthily watch for the helpless;
9   they lurk in secret like a lion in its covert;
  they lurk that they may seize the poor;
  they seize the poor and drag them off in their net.
10 They stoop, they crouch,
  and the helpless fall by their might.
11 They think in their heart, "God has forgotten,
  he has hidden his face, he will never see it." . . .
14 But you do see! Indeed you note trouble and grief,
  that you may take it into your hands;
  the helpless commit themselves to you;
  you have been the helper of the orphan. . . .
17 O LORD, you will hear the desire of the meek;
  you will strengthen their heart, you will incline your ear

^{18} to do justice for the orphan and the oppressed,
    so that those from earth may strike terror no more.

Psalm 80: We've Suffered a Defeat

^{1} Give ear, O Shepherd of Israel,
    you who lead Joseph like a flock! . . .
^{4} O Lord God of hosts,
    how long will you be angry with your people's prayers?
^{5} You have fed them with the bread of tears,
    and given them tears to drink in full measure. . . .
^{8} You brought a vine out of Egypt;
    you drove out the nations and planted it.
^{9} You cleared the ground for it;
    it took deep root and filled the land.
^{10} The mountains were covered with its shade,
    the mighty cedars with its branches;
^{11} it sent out its branches to the sea,
    and its shoots to the River.
^{12} Why then have you broken down its walls,
    so that all who pass along the way pluck its fruit?
^{13} The boar from the forest ravages it,
    and all that move in the field feed on it.
^{14} Turn again, O God of hosts;
    look down from heaven, and see;
    have regard for this vine,
^{15} the stock that your right hand planted.
^{16} They have burned it with fire, they have cut it down;
    may they perish at the rebuke of your countenance.
^{17} But let your hand be upon the one at your right hand,
    the one whom you made strong for yourself.
^{18} Then we will never turn back from you;
    give us life, and we will call on your name.
^{19} Restore us, O Lord God of hosts;
    let your face shine, that we may be saved.

10 minutes
Choose questions according to your interest and time.

1 Who is praying in each of these psalms?

2 How would you summarize the main point each psalm is trying to express?

3 In each psalm, how would you describe the psalmist's mood and attitude?

4 In light of Psalm 10:14, why does the psalmist give God a lengthy description of problems?

5 What assumptions do the psalmists make about the kind of person God is?

6 Why do the psalmists think God should respond to their appeals?

A Guide to the Reading

If participants have not read this section already, read it aloud. Otherwise go on to "Questions for Application."

P salm 96 declared, "The LORD is king!" (96:10). But often God's dominion is difficult to see. Where is God when wealthy people exploit the poor, or a ruthless nation defeats and occupies a weaker neighbor?

The Christian answer, in part, is that God is working in hidden ways to accomplish greater good for those who suffer, if not in this life then in the next. The people who wrote the psalms, however, were generally unaware of a greater life after this earthly one. If God was going to do justice, it would have to be in this present world. So they cried out to God to act here and now for the victims of injustice. Although as Christians we have received more insight into eternity than the Israelites, their prayers for justice can still teach us a great deal.

In Psalm 10 the problem is oppression of the poor. The psalmist is vague on details, describing the situation poetically rather than journalistically. But the word *murder* shows that the situation is grave (10:8). In Psalm 80 Israel has lost a war. The enemy has pillaged the land, undoubtedly killing and enslaving many people. The psalmist speaks of the Israelite nation as a grapevine that God transplanted from Egypt to Canaan. The vine flourished for a while, but now God lets enemies ravage it.

These are prayers of protest. We may imagine the Israelites praying them loudly, tearfully (80:5). The community is grieved not only by their suffering but also by God's seeming indifference.

Even though the prayers challenge God, they are not disrespectful and certainly not lacking in faith. On the contrary, the protests are based on trust. The psalmists cry out to God so demandingly because they are sure God has bound himself to them in a close relationship. They are like family members who know they can raise their voices on occasion without calling their love for each other into question (I am reminded of my Italian grandparents).

Biblical scholar Bernhard Andersen writes that in the psalms "we do not find people shaking their fists in protest at a cold and brassy heaven or resigning themselves grimly to impersonal fate, but people who testify, even in times when they walk through the valley of the dark shadow, that God is faithful and concerned and therefore hears their cry." The psalmists never give up on God. No matter how bad things get, they keep on speaking to him.

In Psalms 10 and 80 we hear people wrestling with God: "Why do you hide yourself in times of trouble?" (10:1). "Why then have you broken down its walls?" (80:12). But the psalmists are not probing the philosophical question of how there can be suffering in a world ruled by a powerful, loving God. They leave that to Job. The psalmists don't want answers; they want action! Their whys are not inquiries in a classroom discussion but cries for help in an emergency room.

The psalmists try to persuade God to act. They appeal to his concern for his reputation: "Look, God," they say, "there is a contradiction between our terrible situation and your love and power. If you don't resolve this contradiction, people will think you don't care. Or they will think that you are powerless. Your good name is at stake" (see 10:4, 11). The psalmists also appeal to God's compassion: "Take a look at this terrible suffering. Surely you can't refrain from doing something about it." Thus the psalmists try to talk God into doing what they want, but they base their appeal on what *God* wants: "We know you are just — so bring justice! We know you are merciful — so show mercy!" To paraphrase Jesus' words: "May *your* kingdom come, may *your* will be done!"

As Christians, we recognize that God may use pain in ways that the Israelite psalmists did not understand. The God who worked through Jesus' cross also works through our sufferings to purify our faith, hope, and love. Nevertheless, as scholar James Luther Mays writes, "God's royal policy against wickedness is never, ever, at any place in Scripture, revised or revoked." God remains just. He continues to care passionately about our earthly well-being and wants us to have the same concern for each other. Psalm 10 can give us words with which to pray insistently and trustingly for God to aid those who suffer injustice. Psalm 80 can express our prayers for God's people, the Church, in whatever injuries the Church suffers from outsiders — and from sins within.

Questions for Application

40 minutes
Choose questions according to your interest and time.

1 To whom might the description of oppression in Psalm 10 apply in today's world?

2 In your prayers, how often do you ask God to bring justice where there is oppression or exploitation? How could you make this request a larger part of your prayers? What could you do to complement your prayer for justice with action?

3 Recall the obstacles facing the Church that you raised in answering "Questions to Begin." How might you use Psalm 80 to ask God to deal with these difficulties?

4 When God seems distant from the world's problems, do you continue to call out to him with faith, expressing your distress to him? Or do you stop praying? Why?

5 What can you learn about how to pray from these two psalms?

6 What line or lines from these psalms would you like to add to your own prayer? Why?

Two recommendations for Bible discussion participants: "Love each member just as she or he is today. Share only what God is revealing to you about yourself and your own life today."

Dorothy King and Kay Murdy, *Guidelines for Catholic Bible Institute*

Approach to Prayer

15 minutes
Use this approach — or create your own!

✦ Recalling your discussion in "Questions to Begin," use Psalm 80 to pray about the obstacles and difficulties facing your parish:

Pray Psalm 80 aloud together.

When you come to the end of the psalm, let each individual member pray, "Lord, take care of this need that we your people have," and then name one of the needs you discussed.

After each need let the whole group respond, "Restore us, O Lord God of hosts; let your face shine, that we may be saved" (80:19).

When you are finished praying for the list of needs, end with the Our Father.

Saints in the Making

Dorothy Day and the Psalms in Jail

This section is a supplement for individual reading.

Dorothy Day, who died in 1980, founded the Catholic Worker movement with Peter Maurin. The following is her recollection of a time spent in jail after a political protest:

Do you know the Psalms? They were what I read most when I was in jail in Occoquan. I read with a sense of coming back to something that I had lost. There was an echoing in my heart. And how can anyone who has known human sorrow and human joy fail to respond to these words? . . .

"Hear, O Lord, my prayer: give ear to my supplication in thy truth: hear me in thy justice. . . . For the enemy hath persecuted my soul: he hath brought down my life to the earth. He hath made me to dwell in darkness . . . and my spirit is in anguish within me. . . ."

All through those weary first days in jail when I was in solitary confinement, the only thoughts that brought comfort to my soul were those lines in the Psalms that expressed the terror and misery of man suddenly stricken and abandoned. Solitude and hunger and weariness of spirit—these sharpened my perceptions so that I suffered not only my own sorrow but the sorrows of those about me. I was no longer myself. I was man. I was no longer a young girl, part of a radical movement seeking justice for those oppressed, I was the oppressed. I was that drug addict, screaming and tossing in her cell, beating her head against the wall. I was that shoplifter who for rebellion was sentenced to solitary. I was that woman who had killed her children, who had murdered her lover. . . .

It has often seemed to me that most people instinctively protect themselves from being touched too closely by the suffering of others. . . . But one who has accepted hardship and poverty as the way of life in which to walk, lays himself open to this susceptibility to the sufferings of others.

And yet if it were not the Holy Spirit that comforted me, how could I have been comforted, how could I have endured, how could I have lived in hope?

GIVE US THIS DAY OUR DAILY BREAD

Question to Begin

15 minutes
Use this question to prepare for the reading and discussion.

✦   What one or two needs in your life do you particularly want God to take care of? Make a list of the group's needs and hold on to it for later in the discussion.

5 minutes
Read the psalms aloud. Let individuals pray successive verses,
or divide into two groups and pray the verses alternately.

Help!

Conversation with God takes the form of both private and community prayer. The model that Jesus fashioned for us is a community prayer: "*Our* Father." Thus we began with psalms prayed by the community of faith (Weeks 1 and 2). This week we shift to reading psalms that are prayers of individuals. Having focused on God and his agenda for the world ("Hallowed by thy name," "Thy kingdom come"), we now bring our personal needs to God.

The Reading

Psalm 5: I'm Falsely Accused

1 Give ear to my words, O LORD;
      give heed to my sighing.
2 Listen to the sound of my cry,
      my King and my God,
      for to you I pray.
3 O LORD, in the morning you hear my voice;
      in the morning I plead my case to you, and watch.
4 For you are not a God who delights in wickedness;
      evil will not sojourn with you.
5 The boastful will not stand before your eyes;
      you hate all evildoers.
6 You destroy those who speak lies;
      the LORD abhors the bloodthirsty and deceitful.
7 But I, through the abundance of your steadfast love,
      will enter your house,
   I will bow down toward your holy temple
      in awe of you.
8 Lead me, O LORD, in your righteousness
      because of my enemies;
      make your way straight before me.
9 For there is no truth in their mouths;
      their hearts are destruction;
   their throats are open graves;

they flatter with their tongues.
10 Make them bear their guilt, O God;
    let them fall by their own counsels;
  because of their many transgressions cast them out,
    for they have rebelled against you.
11 But let all who take refuge in you rejoice;
    let them ever sing for joy.
  Spread your protection over them,
    so that those who love your name may exult in you.
12 For you bless the righteous, O Lord;
    you cover them with favor as with a shield.

Psalm 6: My Pain Is Too Much for Me

1 O Lord, do not rebuke me in your anger,
    or discipline me in your wrath.
2 Be gracious to me, O Lord, for I am languishing;
    O Lord, heal me, for my bones are shaking with terror.
3 My soul also is struck with terror,
    while you, O Lord — how long?
4 Turn, O Lord, save my life;
    deliver me for the sake of your steadfast love.
5 For in death there is no remembrance of you;
    in Sheol who can give you praise?
6 I am weary with my moaning;
    every night I flood my bed with tears;
    I drench my couch with my weeping.
7 My eyes waste away because of grief;
    they grow weak because of all my foes.
8 Depart from me, all you workers of evil,
    for the Lord has heard the sound of my weeping.
9 The Lord has heard my supplication;
    the Lord accepts my prayer.
10 All my enemies shall be ashamed and struck with terror;
    they shall turn back, and in a moment be put to shame.

10 minutes
Choose questions according to your interest and time.

1 Who is speaking in each of these psalms? Is anyone else present?

2 Can you detect anything about when and where either of the psalms is prayed?

3 What problem is the psalmist dealing with in each psalm? How specific is it possible to be about the nature of the psalmist's problem?

4 In each psalm, what is the psalmist's attitude toward his situation?

5 What reasons do the psalmists give God for answering their requests? (Look for statements that begin with words such as *because, for, since, so that,* or *therefore.*)

6 Is there a turning point, a shift of mood, in either of the psalms? If so, what seems to cause it?

A Guide to the Reading

*If participants have not read this section already, read it aloud.
Otherwise go on to "Questions for Application."*

In the psalms of individuals in distress, the sufferers ventilate their pain quite freely. They cry out (5:2), moan, and weep (6:6). They acknowledge — they parade — their suffering without any false stoicism (6:2 – 3, 6 – 7). These people are in trouble, not denial!

The psalmists speak to God in a human way. They know that God is aware of their situation (10:14), but they describe it for him anyway. God does not have a hearing problem (5:3), but when bad things are happening, it seems necessary to get his attention (5:1 – 2).

For all the psalmists' expressiveness, it is not easy to tell just what their problems are. The person praying Psalm 5 faces lying enemies (5:6, 9). But are they spreading malicious gossip or bringing false accusations in court? At first the person praying Psalm 6 seems to suffer from a disease (6:2), but then one wonders whether the psalmist's condition may not reflect depression over enemies' cruelty (6:6 – 7).

The psalms are deliberately nonspecific about the problems at hand, for they were designed to be used by a wide variety of people. These are fill-in-the-blank prayers: you can fit the details of your own circumstances into the psalms' descriptions of woe. The psalmists voice their pain in the common human language of groaning and tears, so their prayers are accessible to us even after twenty-five centuries. "O LORD, give heed to my sighing" (5:1) — I can say that today, without any adjustment.

These psalmists are angry; they call for the destruction of enemies (5:10; 6:10). In one sense, the psalmists' anger reflects opposition to wrongdoing. Sin is hateful, and both God and the psalmists hate it. The psalmists' desire for justice is commendable. At the same time, the gusto with which they envision their enemies' downfall is not commendable. Jesus guides us to "forgive those who trespass against us," rather than demand their punishment — an approach that he himself practiced (Luke 23:34). Yet Christians have continued to use these psalms to express a longing for justice while finding ways to put a Christian spin on the implacable attitude toward enemies. There are three traditional strategies:

✦ Jesus taught the people of his day that their ultimate enemies were not the Roman oppressors but the spiritual powers of evil. In the Lord's Prayer, "deliver us from evil" can be translated "deliver us from the Evil One," that is, from Satan. We can pray the psalms not against human enemies but against the spiritual powers that try to lead us and our enemies away from God.

✦ The fourth-century biblical scholar St. Jerome noted that God opposes all who *are doing* evil (5:5) — not those who have repented. So St. Jerome used the psalms against enemies as appeals to God to give the grace of conversion to evildoers. God seeks to destroy his enemies by making them his friends.

✦ Our most serious enemy is our own tendency to sin. We can pray harsh lines like Psalm 5:8 – 10 in regard to our inclination to evil: "O God, strike down my sinful ways! Crush my bad habits!"

Carmelite scholar Roland Murphy points out that while Christians cannot approve of vengefulness toward enemies, we are nevertheless sometimes deeply angry with other people. Father Murphy suggests that expressing our anger frankly to God, as the psalmists do, may make it easier to relinquish our anger into God's hands.

The reader may wonder where, among the psalmists' appeals for God's help, is the note of submission to God's will. There seems to be no "let it be with me according to your word" (Luke 1:38), whether that means healing or sickness, success or failure.

Yet the psalms may help us abandon ourselves to God's will. In Gethsemane Jesus prayed, much like the psalmists, "My Father, if it is possible, let this cup pass from me." Only after this honest expression of human reluctance to suffer did he pray, "Yet not what I want but what you want" (Matthew 26:39).

During Jesus' life on earth he surely prayed Psalms 5 and 6. As we pray these psalms in suffering and need, Jesus prays them with us. He shares with us his trust in the Father, his expectation that God will ultimately save us from all evil, even from death, as his Father brought him through suffering and death into eternal life. Thus these psalms can help us trustingly surrender to God's will for us.

Questions for Application

40 minutes
Choose questions according to your interest and time.

1 The psalmists express their pain to God freely. Is this a good way to pray? Why or why not? Is there something you might gain from their example?

2 Psalm 5 is an anguished cry against injustice, especially hurtful speech. Is there anyone who might pray Psalm 5 about you? If so, what can you do to be reconciled to that person?

3 Do you know someone who might find Psalm 6 an appropriate prayer? What might you do to comfort that person?

4 If these two psalms are fill-in-the-blank prayers, how might you fill in the blanks?

5 When you find it difficult to accept God's will, do you talk to him about it? say nice prayers without dealing with God honestly? walk away in anger or fear?

6 Who are you angry at? Have you spoken with God about it? Have you left the problem in his hands to work out? Have you asked God to enable you to forgive? Have you prayed for the person you are angry at?

In studying a section of Scripture, "you should observe the fabric — don't study the threads." Each section "should have a main truth, and it shouldn't take weeks to find it."

Norma Spande, *Your Guide to Successful Home Bible Studies*

Approach to Prayer

15 minutes
Use this approach — or create your own!

✦ Employ one of the psalms
to pray for the personal needs
that surfaced in your discussion
of "Question to Begin":

Pray Psalm 5 or 6 aloud
together.

When you come to the end of
the psalm, let individual members pray, "Lord, take care of
this need," and then name one
of the needs you discussed.

After each need let the whole
group respond, "Give ear to my
words, O Lord; give heed to my
sighing" (5:1).

When you are finished praying
for the list of needs, end with
the Our Father.

Saints in the Making

The Psalms in the Life of St. Elizabeth Seton

This section is a supplement for individual reading.

In 1963 Elizabeth Seton became the first person born in the United States to be declared a saint by the Catholic Church. Born in 1774, she grew up in New York City, married a man in the import-export business, and bore five children. Raised an Episcopalian, Elizabeth was familiar with the psalms, and her letters show that she turned to them at the high and low points of life.

Her husband, William, contracted tuberculosis, and in 1803 the couple decided to make a trip to Italy for his health. A quarantine of all U.S. passengers in the port where they arrived forced them to spend a month in prisonlike confinement — just the opposite of the environment William needed. Elizabeth kept their spirits up by reading the psalms aloud. "Often when he hears me repeat the psalms of triumph in God," she wrote, "it so enlivens his spirit that he also makes them his own, and all our sorrows are turned into joy."

William soon died, but Elizabeth's visit to Italy brought her in contact with Catholicism. When she returned to New York, she went through a period of soul-searching over whether to become a Catholic. During this time, she wrote, a "painful and sorrowful . . . impression is left on my heart, it is all clouded and troubled. So I say the penitential psalms, if not with the spirit of the royal prophet [David], at least with his tears . . . yet with such confidence in God that it seems to me he never was so truly my Father."

Within a year Elizabeth made up her mind to enter the Catholic Church. After her first reception of communion as a Catholic she wrote, "To the last breath of life will I not remember this night of watching for morning dawn?" When Jesus entered "the poor little dwelling so all his own," Elizabeth wrote, "the first thought I remember, was, let God arise let his enemies be scattered [Psalm 68:1], for it seemed to me my king had come to take his throne."

FORGIVE US OUR TRESPASSES

Questions to Begin

15 minutes
Use these questions to get warmed up for the reading.

1 Recall a scene from a movie or a book or a soap opera or the Bible in which someone acknowledges they have done something wrong. How would you evaluate their confession?
❑ Too little
❑ Too late
❑ Insincere
❑ A constructive first step
❑ A source of healing and reconciliation
❑ An example to be learned from

2 What reasons would you give for your assessment of the incident?

5 minutes
Read the psalms aloud. Let individuals pray successive verses,
or divide into two groups and pray the verses alternately.

Brokenhearted but Not Despairing

Of the many psalms that cry out to God for help, a handful focus
on the problem of the psalmists' own sins. Traditionally these are
identified as penitential psalms (6; 32; 38; 51; 102; 130; 143).
This week we will read two. These profound prayers can guide us
in expressing our own "forgive us our trespasses" to God.

The Reading

Psalm 51: Lord, Make Me Clean

To the leader. A Psalm of David, when the prophet Nathan came to
him, after he had gone in to Bathsheba.

1 Have mercy on me, O God,
    according to your steadfast love;
  according to your abundant mercy
    blot out my transgressions.
2 Wash me thoroughly from my iniquity,
    and cleanse me from my sin.
3 For I know my transgressions,
    and my sin is ever before me.
4 Against you, you alone, have I sinned,
    and done what is evil in your sight,
  so that you are justified in your sentence
    and blameless when you pass judgment.
5 Indeed, I was born guilty,
    a sinner when my mother conceived me.
6 You desire truth in the inward being;
    therefore teach me wisdom in my secret heart.
7 Purge me with hyssop, and I shall be clean;
    wash me, and I shall be whiter than snow.
8 Let me hear joy and gladness;
    let the bones that you have crushed rejoice.
9 Hide your face from my sins,
    and blot out all my iniquities.
10 Create in me a clean heart, O God,

and put a new and right spirit within me.
11 Do not cast me away from your presence,
    and do not take your holy spirit from me.
12 Restore to me the joy of your salvation,
    and sustain in me a willing spirit.
13 Then I will teach transgressors your ways,
    and sinners will return to you.
14 Deliver me from bloodshed, O God,
    O God of my salvation,
    and my tongue will sing aloud of your deliverance.
15 O Lord, open my lips,
    and my mouth will declare your praise.
16 For you have no delight in sacrifice;
      if I were to give a burnt offering, you would not be
        pleased.
17 The sacrifice acceptable to God is a broken spirit;
      a broken and contrite heart, O God, you will not
        despise. . . .

Psalm 130: Waiting, Waiting for God

1 Out of the depths I cry to you, O LORD.
2   Lord, hear my voice!
    Let your ears be attentive
      to the voice of my supplications!
3 If you, O LORD, should mark iniquities,
    Lord, who could stand?
4 But there is forgiveness with you,
    so that you may be revered.
5 I wait for the LORD, my soul waits,
    and in his word I hope;
6 my soul waits for the LORD
      more than those who watch for the morning,
      more than those who watch for the morning.
7 O Israel, hope in the LORD!
    For with the LORD there is steadfast love,
      and with him is great power to redeem.
8 It is he who will redeem Israel
    from all its iniquities.

10 minutes
Choose questions according to your interest and time.

1 Who is speaking in each of these psalms? Who is present?

2 What is the problem the psalmists are dealing with? What do the psalmists want God to do about it?

3 Why are the psalmists confident that God will forgive them?

4 What picture of God emerges from these two psalms? Cite specific verses to support your statements.

5 Do these psalms suggest that there are elements or stages in our being reconciled with God? If so, what are they?

6 According to these psalms, what is God's part in our reconciliation with him? What is our part?

A Guide to the Reading

If participants have not read this section already, read it aloud.
Otherwise go on to "Questions for Application."

Psalm 51 is the most profound confession of sin in the Bible. After the psalm was composed, a Bible editor, putting it into the collection of psalms, supplied an explanatory heading: "A Psalm of David, when the prophet Nathan came to him, after he had gone in to Bathsheba." The editor connected the psalm with one of the darkest crimes in the Bible (2 Samuel 11). King David committed adultery with Bathsheba, the wife of Uriah, one of his military officers. David then cold-bloodedly arranged to have Uriah killed. The editor's heading cues us that Psalm 51 is a prayer to pray when we have fallen into the worst sins—as well as into lesser ones.

Like Psalms 5 and 6, this is the prayer of an individual in distress. As in those psalms, the psalmist describes his pain to the Lord. But here the pain comes not from the attacks of enemies or the ravages of illness but from the awareness of his own sin, the torment of guilt (51:3). The psalmist has sinned against the very God who has been so faithful to him (51:4).

The psalmist employs a rich imagery to express his* hope that God will forgive his sin: blotting out, washing, cleansing, purging (51:1, 2, 7, 9). But Psalm 51 is an incomparable expression of repentance not so much for its wealth of images as for two other elements.

First, the psalmist makes a straightforward acknowledgment of his sin (51:4). No excuses. No weasel words. No blaming others. No blaming God. The psalmist says, "You, God, are in the right; I am in the wrong." Period.

Verse 5 does not soften this admission of guilt. The psalmist is not saying, "Go easy on me because I can't help sinning: I inherited the problem from my parents." Rather he is saying, "You want me to be a person of integrity, but I have been a sinful person from the first moment of my existence. So you must put your wisdom in my inner being." If God wants us to be different, God will have to change us.

* I am referring to the psalm writers as men since, as far as scholars can determine, virtually all of the authors were men, although obviously both men and women have always used the psalms. But at least one psalm may have been written by a woman (see page 67).

Second, the psalmist cries out for transformation. "Create in me a clean heart, O God" (51:10). Just as God brought a world of light, order, and fruitfulness out of the chaos of dark oceans (Genesis 1), may he now make a person of goodness and faithfulness out of the mess that the psalmist is. Knowing his sinful condition, the psalmist realizes he needs God to act as powerfully as when God created the universe — a tall order! But the psalmist trusts that God will do it. Confidence in God's creative mercy carries him beyond mere relief at forgiveness: he looks forward to joy (51:8, 12, 14 – 15).

Trust in God's mercy is also the keynote of Psalm 130. Here the psalmist thinks in terms of redemption, or ransom, by God. Sins and their bitter consequences are too powerful for the psalmist to escape by himself. But he believes that God will rescue him from these self-produced evils.

Like other psalmists who cry out for God's help, the composers of these two psalms offer God reasons why he should answer their pleas. Significantly, they do not argue that God should hear them because of their sincerity ("This time I'm really, *really* sorry"). Certainly they seem to be truly repentant. But they do not make their repentance the basis of their appeal. Perhaps this is because they know their weakness, their capacity for insincerity: today they are sorry, but tomorrow they may go astray again. They do not present God with a heart restored and ready to do his will, but with a heart broken and needing to be fixed (51:17). Their appeal is not based on anything having to do with themselves, but only on God: "Have mercy on me, O God, according to your steadfast love; according to your abundant mercy" (51:1). Because God is merciful, the psalmists are sure he will not reject the offering of a contrite — that is, crushed — heart (51:17).

Through Jesus, God does indeed heal our hearts. Psalms 51 and 130, as well as prophecies such as Jeremiah 31:33 and Ezekiel 36:26, taught Israel to expect that when God brought his kingdom, he would make their hearts new by his Spirit. Through Jesus, by the power of his Spirit, God is indeed ready to make us new (see Hebrews 8:1 – 12; 10:11 – 25).

Questions for Application

40 minutes
Choose questions according to your interest and time.

---

1 What does the psalmist mean when he speaks of his bones being crushed (51:8), his spirit being broken (51:17)? What experience have you had that helps you understand how the psalmist feels? Are there things in us that have to be broken before we can be made whole?

---

2 What excuses are you inclined to make for your sins? What helps you be honest with God about your sins?

---

3 When you sin, what gives you confidence that God will forgive you?

---

4 What is the main message that you hear in these psalms?

5 How might the psalmists' attitude or way of praying be an example for you?

6 How does the realization of your own sinfulness affect the ways you relate to those who have offended you?

"Avoid 'guide dependency.' . . . Most have experienced the situation where some good momentum is happening in the group discussion of a passage, and someone interrupts with, 'We skipped question 12.'"

Dan Williams, *Starting (& Ending) a Small Group*

Approach to Prayer

15 minutes
Use this approach — or create your own!

✦ Have someone read aloud
Matthew 22:36 – 40.

Then as a group pray either
Psalm 51 or 130 aloud slowly,
pausing for silent reflection
between each verse.

End with the Our Father.

Saints in the Making

Overwhelmed by God's Mercy

This section is a supplement for individual reading.

Margaret Kennedy, of Columbus, Ohio, remembers when "God was barely a part of my day-to-day life." Oh, she prayed sometimes, especially for particular needs. She went to Sunday Mass, though "more out of habit than desire." She managed some Scripture study — "if and when I ever had the time." But one thing Margaret studiously avoided: the sacrament of reconciliation. "I was in a state of denial about how sin affected my life and duly suppressed any guilt that nagged at me over my sins." But then, wanting to become certified to teach in Catholic elementary schools, Margaret began taking some required courses in basic theology.

I was gradually introduced to the idea that maybe God needed to play a more significant part in my life. It became harder to suppress the guilt. Then in class one day, while studying the sacrament of reconciliation, I saw a movie version of the prodigal son (Luke 15:11 – 32). No longer could I remain in denial about my life as a sinner.

By this time I was reading three chapters of Scripture a day, including a psalm. When I came to Psalm 51, I realized I was fooling only myself about my sins. I entered into a tearful prayer with God. Afterwards, though I knew God had forgiven me, I didn't feel quite right. I came to realize that I could not escape availing myself of the sacrament of reconciliation. Reluctant at first, I eventually made an appointment with a priest I trusted.

In my tearful prayer I was overwhelmed with God's mercy and forgiveness. Since then my life has changed. God is an intimate part of every day through prayer, Scripture, and the sacraments. And Psalm 51 — especially verses 12 and 14 — continues to provide help for my greatest daily challenge: loving God, self, and neighbor.

THANK YOU, LORD

Questions to Begin

15 minutes
Use a question or two to get warmed up for the reading.

1 What different ways are there of saying thank you to other people?

2 What is your preferred way of showing your thanks?

3 When have you been especially glad to be thanked? Why was it so important to you?

4 How are you affected when your kindness or efforts to serve seem unappreciated?

5 minutes
Read the psalms aloud. Let individuals pray successive verses,
or divide into two groups and pray the verses alternately.

Adding to the Our Father

The Our Father contains no explicit words of thanks. But it makes sense to thank God when he blesses or helps us. It was certainly part of Jesus' prayers (Matthew 15:36; Luke 10:21; John 11:41; 1 Corinthians 11:23 – 24). And the early Christians gave the Our Father a concluding note of thanksgiving by adding, "For yours is the kingdom, the power, and the glory forever." So let's look at two psalms of thanks.

The Reading

Psalm 30: When I Prayed, God Helped Me

¹ I will extol you, O LORD, for you have drawn me up,
and did not let my foes rejoice over me.
² O LORD my God, I cried to you for help,
and you have healed me.
³ O LORD, you brought up my soul from Sheol,
restored me to life from among those gone down to the
Pit.
⁴ Sing praises to the LORD, O you his faithful ones,
and give thanks to his holy name.
⁵ For his anger is but for a moment;
his favor is for a lifetime. . . .
⁶ As for me, I said in my prosperity,
"I shall never be moved."
⁷ By your favor, O LORD,
you had established me as a strong mountain;
you hid your face;
I was dismayed.
⁸ To you, O LORD, I cried,
and to the LORD I made supplication:
⁹ "What profit is there in my death,
if I go down to the Pit?
Will the dust praise you?
Will it tell of your faithfulness?
¹⁰ Hear, O LORD, and be gracious to me!
O LORD, be my helper!"

¹¹ You have turned my mourning into dancing;
   you have taken off my sackcloth
   and clothed me with joy,
¹² so that my soul may praise you and not be silent.
   O LORD my God, I will give thanks to you forever.

Psalm 92: It's a Pleasure to Remember What God Has Done

¹ It is good to give thanks to the LORD,
   to sing praises to your name, O Most High;
² to declare your steadfast love in the morning,
   and your faithfulness by night,
³ to the music of the lute and the harp,
   to the melody of the lyre.
⁴ For you, O LORD, have made me glad by your work;
   at the works of your hands I sing for joy.
⁵ How great are your works, O LORD!
   Your thoughts are very deep!
⁶ The dullard cannot know,
   the stupid cannot understand this:
⁷ though the wicked sprout like grass
   and all evildoers flourish,
  they are doomed to destruction forever,
⁸   but you, O LORD, are on high forever.
⁹ For your enemies, O LORD,
   for your enemies shall perish;
   all evildoers shall be scattered.
¹⁰ But you have exalted my horn like that of the wild ox;
   you have poured over me fresh oil.
¹¹ My eyes have seen the downfall of my enemies;
   my ears have heard the doom of my evil assailants.
¹² The righteous flourish like the palm tree,
   and grow like a cedar in Lebanon.
¹³ They are planted in the house of the LORD;
   they flourish in the courts of our God.
¹⁴ In old age they still produce fruit;
   they are always green and full of sap,
¹⁵ showing that the LORD is upright;
   he is my rock, and there is no unrighteousness in him.

10 minutes
Choose questions according to your interest and time.

---

1   Who is speaking in these
    psalms?

---

2   Who is listening?

---

3   What differences in tone do you
    notice between the two psalms?
    What aspects of thanksgiving
    does each psalm emphasize?

---

4   Which verses explain why
    the composer of Psalm 30
    praises God?

---

5   How could the three Christian
    interpretations of the word
    enemies, as found on pages
    36 – 37, be applied to the refer-
    ences to enemies in Psalm 92?

A Guide to the Reading

If participants have not read this section already, read it aloud. Otherwise go on to "Questions for Application."

When the psalmists cry out to God in suffering, they constantly remind God that he and the psalmist are in a lifetime relationship: "You are my God" (Psalm 143:10; see also 25:5; 31:14; 40:17; 70:5; 86:2; 140:6; 141:8). Since God has bound himself to them in a deeply personal way, the psalmists argue, surely he ought to come through for them when they are in dire need.

The psalmists are aware of their bond with God not only when they need his help. When God lifts them up out of their troubles, the psalmists do not just brush themselves off and go on with life. They make a visit to a nearby shrine or the temple in Jerusalem and thank him by praying a psalm. Along with their prayer they might also offer an animal sacrifice, using some of the meat for a festive meal with their family and friends. Psalms 30 and 92 are texts for such occasions.

In the psalms of thanks, the psalmists generally say something about the distress they were in. The writer of Psalm 30 gives a rather vague description (30:2–3). Was he sick? injured? At any rate, the imagery indicates that the situation was life threatening. The Israelites thought the dead descended to a gloomy realm under the earth ("Sheol" — 30:3). The burial tunnels and water-holding cisterns that the Israelites dug in the ground seemed like entryways into this dark realm. The psalmist felt as though he had fallen into one of these burial shafts or cisterns ("Pit" — 30:3). He seemed to have little chance of seeing the light of day again. But God hauled him up like a bucket of water from a well (30:3). To the psalmist, his recovery feels like a resurrection ("[you] restored me to life" — 30:3).

By contrast, the psalmist of Psalm 92 refers to his former distress only indirectly (apparently he had enemies — 92:11). And he mentions God's help only briefly (92:11).

Differences like these give the various psalms of thanks their distinctive flavors. We can choose those psalms that suit us best.

Whatever divine rescue the author of Psalm 92 experienced, God's intervention filled him with a tremendous sense of well-being (92:10 – 15). He feels as strong as an ox (92:10). He is confident that he will go on being vigorous into old age, like a palm that stays leafy and bears juicy dates (92:14).

The thankful psalmists often recount how they prayed for God's help. For example, the composer of Psalm 30 quotes his earlier prayer (30:8 – 10). For anyone who might be listening, this makes the point that God hears us and answers us when we turn to him.

In fact, the psalmists address their words not only to God but also to their companions and to any bystanders in the temple courtyard. This action reflects their understanding of thanksgiving, because the Hebrew word for thanks, as in Psalms 30:4 and 92:1, literally means "acknowledge" or "give voice to." The same Hebrew word is used in Psalm 32:5: "I will confess my transgressions to the Lord," in other words, "I will openly acknowledge my sins." Thanking God involves publicizing what he has done. This aspect of thanksgiving is amplified by another word the psalmists use — the word that is translated "tell" in Psalm 30:9 and "declare" in Psalm 92:2. That Hebrew word means "narrate" or "report."

For the psalmists, then, giving thanks does not mean simply letting God know how much they appreciate his help. It means acknowledging and reporting how God has brought them healing, safety, well-being. They publicize what God has done for them so that other people will see how trustworthy God is and will praise him too — and will turn to him in their own troubles.

Biblical scholar Gerhard von Rad maintains that, for the psalmists, God's action in their lives did not belong just to them but to the community. They would have thought it an incalculable loss if they remained silent and others were not able to profit from what God had done for them. The composers of Psalms 30 and 92 never heard Jesus' instruction to pray that God's name would be hallowed, that is, that God would come to be regarded by everyone as holy, merciful, faithful, and good. Nevertheless, the prayers they composed were designed to accomplish exactly that.

Questions for Application

40 minutes
Choose questions according to your interest and time.

1 Think of an experience you have had of recovering from sickness, getting safely through danger, or overcoming a pattern of sin. Where can you see God's hand in those developments?

2 How do you try to keep fresh the memory of ways that God has helped (rescued, healed, forgiven, changed) you? How often do you recall the ways you have experienced God's help?

3 How do you thank God for his goodness to you? When do you forget to thank him?

4 In what ways do you thank God by letting other people know what God has done for you? How could you do this more?

5 Paul urges us to "give thanks in all circumstances" (1 Thessalonians 5:18), but we cannot constantly have feelings of appreciation. How might the psalmists' approach to thanksgiving shed light on how we can do what Paul says?

6 What modern images might be used to express what the psalmist is trying to say in Psalm 92:10–15?

In Bible discussion, "the listener sets aside the 'internal dialogue' of daydreams and personal planning to focus attention entirely on the speaker. . . . We refrain from taking 'mental vacations' from the conversation."
Barbara J. Fleischer, *Facilitating for Growth*

Approach to Prayer

15 minutes
Use this approach — or create your own!

✦ Use verses from Psalm 92 to
create a litany of thanks:

Go around the group, letting
participants, if they wish,
mention one thing for which
they are grateful to God.
After each item, have the
group pray aloud the following
lines (Psalm 92:1–2):

It is good to give thanks to the
Lord,
to sing praises to your name,
O Most High;
to declare your steadfast love in
the morning,
and your faithfulness by night.

You might go around two or
three times, depending on the
interest and size of the group.

End with the Our Father.

A Living Tradition

St. Bernard of Clairvaux and Psalms of Thanks

This section is a supplement for individual reading.

Bernard of Clairvaux, a twelfth-century French monk, was one of the most admired and influential men in Europe. This excerpt is adapted from the first of his sermons on the Song of Songs.

Consider your own experience. When your faith has given you the victory that overcomes the world and you get out of "the desolate pit, out of the miry bog" (Psalm 40:2), haven't you sung "to the LORD a new song, for he has done marvelous things" (Psalm 98:1)? I think "a song of praise to our God" (Psalm 40:3) for his graces was put in your mouth when he set your "feet upon a rock" and made your steps "secure" (Psalm 40:2) in a new life. When you repented of your sins, God not only forgave you but also promised great rewards. So didn't you rejoice in the hope of good things to come and more than ever "sing of the ways of the LORD, for great is the glory of the LORD" (Psalm 138:5)?

If God clarifies for you a passage in Scripture that was impenetrably dark, then by all means you should give him the pleasure of hearing "glad shouts and songs of thanksgiving" (Psalm 42:4) for the nourishing heavenly bread you have received.

People who are trying to lead a pious life in Christ are never free from daily struggles and attacks by the flesh, the world, and the devil. As you constantly discover that the life of the person on earth is warfare, you should renew a daily song for victories attained. As often as a temptation is overcome, or a bad habit is conquered, or an impending danger is turned aside, or the snare of an ambusher is detected, or some old and long-standing sinful drive is once and for all healed, or a virtue that you have very much wanted and prayed for is at last obtained by some gift of God, shouldn't thanksgiving and praise sound forth? Shouldn't God be blessed for each and every one of his gifts?

FATHER!

Questions to Begin

15 minutes
Use a question or two to get warmed up for the reading.

1 Describe a situation where you found it difficult to trust someone but were glad afterward that you did.

2 Who in your life has been trustworthy and faithful? What has their loyalty meant to you?

Opening the Bible

5 minutes
Read the psalms aloud. Let individuals pray successive verses,
or divide into two groups and pray the verses alternately.

Our Trustworthy God

At the end of our exploration of the book of Psalms, we return
to the beginning of the prayer that has guided our exploration,
to the first words of Jesus' model prayer—"Our Father." Jesus en-
courages us to speak to the creator of the universe as a loving
parent. "Father!" Could there be any way of addressing God that
more clearly expresses our intimacy with him, our dependence on
him, our trust in his love? Among the psalms are some that neither
ask God for help nor thank him for particular blessings but simply
express trust in him. We read two of these psalms this week.

The Reading

Psalm 91: God Will Protect You

> ¹ You who live in the shelter of the Most High,
>   who abide in the shadow of the Almighty,
> ² will say to the LORD, "My refuge and my fortress;
>   my God, in whom I trust."
> ³ For he will deliver you from the snare of the fowler
>   and from the deadly pestilence;
> ⁴ he will cover you with his pinions,
>   and under his wings you will find refuge;
>   his faithfulness is a shield and buckler.
> ⁵ You will not fear the terror of the night,
>   or the arrow that flies by day,
> ⁶ or the pestilence that stalks in darkness,
>   or the destruction that wastes at noonday.
> ⁷ A thousand may fall at your side,
>   ten thousand at your right hand,
>   but it will not come near you.
> ⁸ You will only look with your eyes
>   and see the punishment of the wicked.
> ⁹ Because you have made the LORD your refuge,
>   the Most High your dwelling place,
> ¹⁰ no evil shall befall you,

no scourge come near your tent.
11 For he will command his angels concerning you
    to guard you in all your ways.
12 On their hands they will bear you up,
    so that you will not dash your foot against a stone.
13 You will tread on the lion and the adder,
    the young lion and the serpent you will trample under
    foot.
14 Those* who love me, I will deliver;
    I will protect those who know my name.
15 When they call to me, I will answer them;
    I will be with them in trouble,
    I will rescue them and honor them.
16 With long life I will satisfy them,
    and show them my salvation.

Psalm 131: Peaceful Trust

1 O Lord, my heart is not lifted up,
    my eyes are not raised too high;
I do not occupy myself with things
    too great and too marvelous for me.
2 But I have calmed and quieted my soul,
    like a weaned child with its mother;
    my soul is like the weaned child that is with me.
3 O Israel, hope in the Lord
    from this time on and forevermore.

---

* To avoid using masculine pronouns to refer to both men and women, the translators sometimes replace a singular masculine pronoun in Hebrew *(he, him)* with a plural *(they, them, those)*. In the Hebrew, verses 14 through 16 use the masculine singular pronoun. For example, verse 14 can be translated, "Because he cleaves to me in love, I will deliver him." God's promise is to *each individual person.*

10 minutes
Choose questions according to your interest and time.

1 Who is speaking in each of these psalms? Is the same person speaking all the way through Psalm 91?

2 Who is being spoken to?

3 Psalm 91 compares God to a fortress (91:2). What other images for God does the psalm use? What image does Psalm 131 use for God?

4 Are any of the words in this translation of Psalm 91 unfamiliar to you? If so, look them up in a dictionary, or compare this translation with another one.

5 Is there a logical connection between verses 1 and 2 in Psalm 131?

A Guide to the Reading

If participants have not read this section already, read it aloud. Otherwise go on to "Questions for Application."

In Psalm 91 a person hoping to escape trouble of some sort goes to the temple in Jerusalem. When the person arrives, a priest meets the person at the gate with words of reassurance (91:1 – 13). Someone with a prophetic gift then delivers a promise of divine help, speaking in God's name (91:14 – 16).

The supplicant may have been especially worried about sickness: verses 5 and 6 refer poetically to various diseases. Israelites who prayed this psalm probably thought these afflictions were caused by demons. But the psalm assures the one seeking God's help that God is much greater than such horrible attackers. Indeed, God sends his own more powerful helpers to care for those who trust him (91:11 – 12).

Verse 13 promises that the person who lives under God's protection will overcome all the forces of destruction and chaos in the world. Jesus renewed this sweeping promise to his followers (Luke 10:18 – 19). Having endured death and risen into unending life, Jesus will ultimately restore life and wholeness to us, despite whatever damage we suffer from sin, death, and the powers of darkness. Already in the present world, Jesus in us is greater than the forces of evil we face (see Romans 8:38 – 39; 1 John 5:4).

Perhaps because Jesus adopted the words from this psalm, St. Jerome, the fourth-century biblical scholar, saw Jesus reflected throughout Psalm 91. For example, Jerome wrote about verse 4: "When the Lord was raised up on the cross, he stretched out his hands like a mother eagle stretching out her wings over her young. His hands were raised not to ask God's help for himself but to protect us in our neediness."

The assurance of Psalm 91 comes with a condition. It promises God's protection to the person who makes God his or her refuge (91:9; see also 91:1 – 2, 14 – 15). God is faithful, but to enjoy his faithfulness, it is necessary to respond to him with trust.

Luke's Gospel tells us the devil quoted Psalm 91 to Jesus to persuade him to test God's faithfulness. From the pinnacle of the temple the devil challenged Jesus: "'If you are the Son of God, throw yourself down from here, for it is written, "He will command his angels concerning you, to protect you," and "On their hands they will bear you up, so that you will not dash your foot against a stone."' Jesus answered him, 'It is said, "Do not put the Lord your God to the test"'" (Luke 4:9–12). Jesus' trust in God's care was so great that he did not need to make God prove his love. Thus Jesus gave a perfect example of the trust in God that Psalm 91 speaks of.

Psalm 131 expresses this wholehearted trust in God. Almost all of the psalms seem to have been written by men (although women are responsible for some of the finest poetry elsewhere in the Old Testament — see Exodus 15:20–21; Judges 5; 1 Samuel 2:1–10). But Psalm 131 is written from a woman's point of view, which suggests that a woman was the author. Verse 2 might be translated, "I have calmed and quieted my soul as a just-nursed child resting on its mother's arms; as my just-nursed child rests on me, so I rest in the arms of God."

We may picture a mother looking down at her baby and seeing an image of her own total dependence on God. The peace of this prayer exceeds that of the psalmists who cry out for help, no matter how great their trust in God. Here the psalmist expresses confidence that God already knows all needs and will provide whatever is needed with perfect love.

In the struggles of life, we rightly call on God for help. Yet ultimately we must allow God to decide how and when he will answer our prayers. In times of suffering and sorrow, we pray with Jesus in Gethsemane, "Let this cup pass from me." We ought to continue with him as he prays, "Yet not what I want but what you want" (Matthew 26:39).

Isaac of Nineveh, a sixth-century saint who lived in what is now Iraq, wrote that those who trust God go beyond prayers of "give us this" or "take that away" and leave all their concerns in God's hands. "For at each moment, by the eyes of faith, they see the fatherly providence that gives them the protection of that true Father whose infinite love surpasses all fatherly love. He, more than all, has the power to help us in a measure greater than anything we may ask, think, or conceive."

Questions for Application

40 minutes
Choose questions according to your interest and time.

1   What are you most anxious about?

2   What do the assurances of God's protection in Psalm 91 mean, since we know we live in a world where none of us can escape suffering?

3   If you were to read Psalm 91 as Jesus' personal words to you, what would the message of this psalm be for you?

4 When have you had a moment of peaceful trust in God like that described in Psalm 131? What were the circumstances? When you face difficulties, how could you exercise the faith in God that you had at that moment of peace?

5 How do people grow to trust other people? to trust God?

"Do let the Bible speak for itself. Sometimes all that is necessary is that a passage is read well and with understanding."

Christine Dodd, *Making Scripture Work*

Approach to Prayer

15 minutes
Use this approach — or create your own!

✦ Conclude with prayer in which you express your trust in God and ask him to deepen your trust in him:

Let each person mention one or two areas of life where they are tempted to feel anxious. Then let the rest of the group speak to the person these promises of the Lord (Psalm 91:14 – 16):

Those who love me, I will
    deliver;
  I will protect those who know
    my name.
When they call to me, I will
    answer them;
  I will be with them in trouble,
  I will rescue them and honor
    them.
With long life I will satisfy them,
  and show them my salvation.

After you have gone around the whole group, pray Psalm 131 together. Then end with the Our Father.

A Living Tradition
St. Augustine on Psalm 91:16

This section is a supplement for individual reading.

This excerpt is adapted from a commentary on Psalm 91 by St. Augustine, fifth-century bishop of Hippo, in present-day Tunisia.

"With length of days I will satisfy him" (Psalm 91:16). What is length of days? It is eternal life! Brothers and sisters, don't think "length of days" refers to the kind of days that are shorter in winter and longer in summer. Is that the kind of days God is able to give us? The length spoken of here has no end: it is the eternal life that is promised us.

And because eternal life really does satisfy, it made sense for him to say, "I will satisfy him." Whatever lasts a long time does not satisfy us if it has an end — and for that reason should not even be called long. If we're greedy, we should be greedy for eternal life. Desire the kind of life that has no end! Let that be where our greed is directed. Do you want riches without limit? Then let there be no limit to your desire for eternal life.

"I will show him my salvation." This means, "I will show him Christ himself." But hasn't Christ already been seen on earth? What greater sight can God show us? Christ has not, however, been seen in the way we will see him. He was seen in such a way that those who saw him crucified him, while we who have not seen him have believed in him. They had eyes; we do not, for although we have the eyes of the heart, still we see by faith, not by appearance. When will his appearing be? When we see him "face to face" (1 Corinthians 13:12) with the seeing that God promises us as the great reward of all our exertions.

In everything, then, exert yourself for this: that you may see him. Great beyond knowing is that which we are going to see when our whole reward is our seeing and the great sight we see is our Lord Jesus Christ.

P erhaps you've been praying the psalms for years. But even if the last few weeks were the first time you gave the psalms much attention, you've now explored a dozen of them. This gives you a bridgehead into the book of Psalms from which you can push out into the rest of the book.

For two reasons you're now in a good position to go on getting acquainted with the psalms and making them part of your prayers. First, in this booklet we've looked at six types of psalms: hymns of praise, community appeals for God's help, individual appeals, prayers of repentance, prayers of thanksgiving, and prayers of trust. Most of the remaining 138 psalms fit into one of these six categories, so what you've learned about the dozen psalms in the discussions will help you understand and pray many of the other psalms.

Second, the weekly discussions have used a format that can be applied to any of the psalms. Perhaps without realizing it, you've been learning a method for digging into the psalms just by using this booklet. It may be helpful to review this method in order to clarify how you can employ it as you continue your investigation of the book of Psalms.

Six Steps for Exploring the Psalms

Our discussions have employed a six-step strategy for getting acquainted with a psalm:

Step 1. Pray the psalm aloud. Psalms were made to be sung. As we have seen, they mention musical accompaniment (Psalms 92:1–3; 150). Originally some of them were probably pretty noisy prayers punctuated by shouts and clapping (Psalms 47; 95:1–2). Not only the hymns of praise but also the appeals for help were meant for more than silent reading. The psalmists' cries for help are exactly that — cries, reinforced with a fair amount of moaning and groaning (Psalms 6:6; 88:1). Our own prayers may ordinarily be much more subdued, but voicing the psalms helps bring them to life. It's hard to get the flavor of a passage such as Psalm 96:10 – 13 (Week 1) without at least saying it aloud.

Step 2. Give the psalm a careful second reading. Ask some simple questions to establish clearly in your own mind what is going on in the psalm. In our weekly discussions, questions of this type have been grouped under the heading "Questions for Careful Reading." Among the generally useful questions are these:

+ Who is speaking: an individual? more than one individual? a community? God? Does the speaker change from one part of the psalm to another?

+ Who is being spoken to?

+ Who is present, either literally or in imagination? There is always the psalmist and God, but what about a community? friends? enemies?

+ How would you sum up the message of the psalm?

+ How would you characterize the psalmist's attitude toward his situation: sorrow? weariness? fear? anger? (at whom?) trust? exuberance?

+ Does the psalmist want something? If so, what is it?

+ Is there a shift of mood at any point in the psalm? If so, what seems to cause it?

+ Examine the psalmist's reasoning: (1) If the psalmist is praising and thanking God, what reasons does he give for why God should be praised and thanked? (2) If the psalmist is seeking God's help, what reasons does he give God for helping him? Look for statements that follow words like *for, since, because,* or *so that.*

+ What picture of God emerges from this psalm?

These questions are not necessarily deep or engaging, but they help us notice what the psalmist is actually saying.

Step 3. Look for lines you could easily make a part of your prayers. Ask yourself, What do I like about this psalm? What do I resonate to? Could any of these lines help me express myself to God?

In many cases, something short and uncomplicated may strike you. In Psalm 5, for example, the words that stand out to me are simply "My God . . . to you I pray" (5:2). They remind me of how I prayed after my wife died some years ago. There were moments when I desperately wanted to find some comfort from God, but I was so distraught I had no idea what to say to him. So I would say, "You know, Lord. You know." Or even just, "You, Lord." That was about as much as I could pray. Yet the recognition contained in those words anchored my life — the recognition that God does hear me when I pray.

Step 4. Explore the unfamiliar or puzzling parts of the psalm. We look into the psalms in the hope that they will lead us to pray in new or deeper ways. This will happen only if we let the psalms show us things we don't already know. The parts of the psalms that are strange to us usually have the greatest potential for teaching us. But in order to understand what is strange or confusing, we must put some effort into learning. We do not need to become biblical scholars. But we need to move a little beyond what we already know.

In this booklet, the "Guide to the Reading" section has offered some material for greater understanding. Beyond this booklet, you can find various simple ways to enlarge your knowledge of the book of Psalms. One way is to use a study Bible, that is, an edition that has introductory articles and notes in the margin or at the bottom of the page (see the list at the back of this booklet). Another way is to get a book about Psalms. I recommend C. S. Lewis's *Reflections on the Psalms*. Some other books are mentioned at the end of this article.

Step 5. Ask how the psalm applies to you. Now that you have examined how the psalmist prays, compare his way of praying to your own. What are the differences? Could the psalmist's style of praying, the psalmist's way of reasoning with God, the psalmist's emphasis, teach you something about prayer? How could this psalm lead you to pray differently? For what situations in your own life might you pray this psalm of thanks, this psalm of appeal, or this psalm of trust?

You might review "Questions for Application" in the weekly discussions. Asking these types of questions may help you reflect on how the psalm might have an impact on your own prayer.

Step 6. Pray the psalm again. Praying the psalm is not a onetime step. The goal of working your way through a psalm is to add something to your ongoing conversation with God. So give the psalm a chance to do this. Pray the psalm over and over. Pray it with feeling. The more you pray it, the more you will see in it, and the greater the effect it will have on you.

You are under no obligation to pray the psalm in its entirety. While it is instructive to read and explore the whole psalm, at the end of the process you are free to leave parts of it aside as you integrate it into your prayers. If certain parts seem less useful to you, omit them. Focus on the parts that seem most helpful. This, after all, is what the Church does with psalms in the liturgy. Only a few verses of a psalm are selected for recitation during the liturgy of the Word.

Resources for Exploring the Psalms

✦ Bernhard W. Anderson, *Out of the Depths: The Psalms Speak for Us Today,* rev. ed. (Philadelphia: Westminster John Knox Press, 1995). A seminary professor distills years of study of the book of Psalms into an informative guide for laypeople.

✦ St. Augustine, *Commentary on the Psalms.* Various translations are available. An older version is offered free on the Internet at www.ccel.wheaton.edu under "Early Church Fathers."

✦ C. S. Lewis, *Reflections on the Psalms* (New York: Harcourt Brace Jovanovich, 1958). This penetrating, clearly written book explores the difficulties that may arise as we read the book of Psalms.

Suggestions for Bible Discussion Groups

L ike a camping trip, a Bible discussion group works best if you agree on what you're undertaking together, why you're doing it, where you hope to get to, and how you intend to get there. Many groups use their first meeting to reach a consensus on such questions. Here is a checklist of issues, with a few bits of advice from people with experience in Bible discussions. (A planning discussion will go more smoothly if the leaders have thought through the following issues beforehand.)

Agree on your purpose. Are you getting together to gain wisdom and direction for your life? to finally get acquainted with the Bible? to support one another in following Christ? to encourage those who are exploring — or reexploring — the Church? for other reasons?

Agree on attitudes. For example: "We're all beginners here." "We're here to help each other understand and respond to God's Word." "We're not here to offer counseling or direction to each other." "We want to read Scripture prayerfully." What do *you* wish to emphasize? Make it explicit!

Agree on ground rules. Barbara J. Fleischer, in her useful book *Facilitating for Growth,* recommends that a group clearly state its approach to the following:

+ Preparation. Do we agree to read the material before each meeting?

+ Attendance. What kind of priority will we give to our meetings?

+ Self-revelation. Are we willing to help the others in the group gradually get to know us — our weaknesses as well as our strengths, our needs as well as our gifts?

+ Listening. Will we commit ourselves to listening to each other?

+ Confidentiality. Will we keep everything that is shared with the group in the group?

+ Encouragement and support. Will we give as well as receive?

✦ Participation. Will we work to allow everyone time and opportunity to make a contribution?

You could probably take a pen and draw a circle around *listening* and *confidentiality*. Those two points are especially important.

The following items could be added to Fleischer's list:

✦ Relationship with parish. Is our group part of the religious education program? independent but operating with the express approval of the pastor? not a parish-based group at all?

✦ New members. In the course of the six meetings, will new members be allowed?

Agree on housekeeping.

✦ When will we meet?

✦ How often will we meet? Meeting weekly or every other week is best if you can manage it. William Riley remarks, "Meetings once a month are too distant from each other for the threads of the last session not to be lost" *(The Bible Study Group: An Owner's Manual)*.

✦ How long will meetings run?

✦ Where will we meet?

✦ Is any setup needed? Christine Dodd writes that "the problem with meeting in a place like a church hall is that it can be very soul-destroying" given the cold, impersonal feel of many church facilities. If you have to meet in a church facility, Dodd recommends doing something to make the area homey *(Making Scripture Work)*.

✦ Who will host the meetings? Leaders and hosts are not necessarily identical.

✦ Will we have refreshments? Who will provide them?

77

✦ What about child care? Most experienced leaders of Bible discussion groups discourage bringing infants or other children to adult Bible discussions.

Agree on leadership. You need someone to facilitate—to keep the discussion on track, to see that everyone has a chance to speak, to help the group stay on schedule. Rena Duff, editor of the newsletter *Sharing God's Word Today,* recommends having two or three people take turns leading the discussions.

It's okay if the leader is not an expert regarding the Bible. You have this booklet, and if questions come up that no one can answer, you can delegate a participant to do a little research between meetings. It's important for the leader to set an example of listening, to draw out the quieter members (and occasionally restrain the more vocal ones), to move the group on when it gets stuck, to remind the members of their agreements, and to summarize what the group is accomplishing.

Bible discussion is an opportunity to experience the fulfillment of Jesus' promise "Where two or three are gathered in my name, I am there among them" (Matthew 18:20). Put your discussion group in Jesus' hands. Pray for the guidance of the Spirit. And have a great time exploring God's Word together!

Y ou can use this booklet just as well for individual study as for group discussion. While discussing the Bible with other people can be a rich experience, there are advantages to individual reading. For example:

✦ You can focus on the points that interest you most.

✦ You can go at your own pace.

✦ You can be completely relaxed and unashamedly honest in your answers to all the questions, since you don't have to share them with anyone else!

My suggestions for using this booklet on your own are these:

✦ Don't skip "Questions to Begin." The questions can help you as an individual reader warm up to the topic of the reading.

✦ Take your time on "Questions for Careful Reading" and "Questions for Application." While a group will probably not have enough time to work on all the questions, you can allow yourself the time to consider all of them if you are using the booklet by yourself.

✦ If you are going through the book of Psalms at your own pace, consider reading additional psalms, not just those excerpted in this booklet. The more psalms you read, the greater your total understanding will be.

✦ Since you control the pace, give yourself plenty of opportunities to reflect on the meaning of the psalms for you. Let the psalmists lead you to deeper trust in God. Let your reading of the psalms be an opportunity for these prayers to become your words to God.

Bibles

The following editions of the Bible contain the full set of biblical books recognized by the Catholic Church, along with a great deal of useful explanatory material:

+ The Catholic Study Bible (Oxford University Press), which uses the text of the New American Bible.

+ The Catholic Bible: Personal Study Edition (Oxford University Press), which also uses the text of the New American Bible

+ The New Jerusalem Bible, the regular (not the reader's) edition (Doubleday)

How has Scripture had an impact on your life? Was this booklet helpful to you in your study of the Bible? Please send comments, suggestions, and personal experiences to Kevin Perrotta c/o Trade Editorial Department, Loyola Press, 3441 N. Ashland Ave., Chicago, IL 60657.